Patient
Evangelism

Other Books by Lloyd Pulley

Walk in Love: Following God's Plan for Marriage
(Also available in Spanish, Russian, Hungarian, & French)
ISBN 0-9676414-0-3

Patient Evangelism

reaching the multitudes one at a time

Lloyd Pulley

CALVARY CHAPEL
PUBLISHING

Santa Ana, California

Patient Evangelism
Reaching the Multitudes One at a Time

Copyright © 2003 by Lloyd Pulley

Published by Calvary Chapel Publishing (CCP)
A resource ministry of Calvary Chapel Costa Mesa
3800 South Fairview Road
Santa Ana, CA 92704

ISBN 1-931667-62-4

First printing, 2003

Printed in the United States of America.

Cover photo by: Tom Price
Used by permission of *Calvary Chapel Magazine*

Dedication

To all those who have a passion
to share the love of Christ
in the world today.

Table of Contents

Foreword

A few years ago, as I passed through London's Leicester Square, I noticed that a crowd had gathered around a man who was using a drawing board, which had some sort of a graphic riddle on it, to get people's attention. I stopped just in time to see the riddle solved and was thrilled to find that it concerned Jesus Christ and the salvation that He offers to mankind. The man conducting this evangelistic outreach turned from his drawing board to the crowd, and in some of the harshest tones I've ever heard, began pronouncing damnation upon his audience. As you can imagine, it was only a matter of seconds before the crowd, numbering around fifty people initially, was reduced to about two. I was one of the two.

As I stood there listening to the man rant and rave, I thought to myself, "What a tragedy; this man thinks he's preaching the Gospel, but in reality, he's doing a great disservice to the cause of the Kingdom." At that moment, the man approached me, and in that same harsh tone, asked if I wanted to be saved.

I assured him that I was saved and asked if I might give him a bit of advice based on my observation of his evangelistic method. Although he made it clear that he wasn't interested in what I had to say, even expressing doubts about my salvation, I felt compelled to challenge him about the way he was misrepresenting God.

I began by saying, "Have you ever thought to tell people that God loves them and has a wonderful plan for their lives...?" Before I could go any further, he pronounced me a heretic and stomped off, calling down judgments upon me.

Although this is somewhat of an extreme example of the wrong way to evangelize, I'm afraid this type of thing happens far too often. Just the other day, I saw a man carrying a large wooden cross down a busy street, forcing literature upon people as they passed by. Once again, I couldn't help but think of how unlike Jesus and the Apostles that kind of approach was.

As Christians, we have the great privilege and responsibility of sharing the Gospel with those who don't yet know the Lord. However, we must make sure that we are sharing it in a way that properly represents our Lord. The Apostle Paul, in writing to the church of Thessalonica, said, "We were gentle among you, just as a nursing mother cherishes her own children. So, affectionately longing for you, we were well pleased to impart to you not only the gospel of God, but also our own lives" (1 Thessalonians 2:7-8).

This was Paul's approach to people; this was also the approach of Jesus, who said, "Come to Me, all you who labor and are heavy laden...for

I am gentle and [humble] in heart" (Matthew 11: 28-29).

This is something that Lloyd and I were so powerfully reminded of as we sought to bring hope and peace to the multitudes in New York City whose world had been turned upside down by the events of September 11, 2001.

Patient Evangelism was born out of those experiences. I was tremendously blessed as I read it, and I know you will be too. It is a timely message that reminds us once again that God's love is the greatest power in the universe.

Pastor Brian Brodersen
Calvary Chapel of Costa Mesa

Acknowledgements

To Brian Brodersen. Thank you for the incredible support you were to me personally during such a challenging time. You urged me on to the next step and kept me going forward in the direction that God was leading.

To Tom Price. Your availability and eagerness to document the ministry that was taking place at Ground Zero was an encouragement to the hearts of so many who needed to be reminded that God was still in control.

To Scott and Kerry Hasenbalg. God sent you all the way from Virginia to lead us to the place in New York City where He wanted us to minister. Thank you for heeding His call and for sharing in the work of the Lord with us.

To my staff. What can I say to a group of people who willingly spent hours on the streets of Manhattan in addition to their regular responsibilities? You guys are the best. Thank you for putting up with my wild adventures!

To Carol Eskaros and Noreen Hay. The two very fine and feisty editors who effectively chased

me down and made sure that what I meant was
actually what I said.

To my wife, Karen, who unflinchingly releases
and encourages me to follow the Lord without
reserve.

To my Lord Jesus. You are my all in all!

Share the Gospel

In some of the most familiar passages in the New Testament, Jesus commissions His church to go and make disciples of all nations (Matthew 28: 19) and to be His witnesses in every place and in every generation (Acts 1:8). Indeed, had it not been for the faithfulness and endurance of the saints throughout the ages, you and I may never have learned of God's love for us through His Son, Jesus Christ.

Today, the awesome responsibility of sharing the Gospel with all people has been passed down to our generation. We are now the ones to carry the message of the hope of Christ to the world around us, and we only have a short while in which to do this crucial work.

The questions we must ask ourselves are these: How are we doing? Do those around us know we really care? Are we accurately representing Christ and His love to them?

As a pastor of a church in the New York metropolitan area, these questions became my fervent prayers as we sought to minister in the aftermath of the terrorist attacks of September 11, 2001. The magnitude of this challenge went far beyond anything we had ever encountered before as a body of believers. More than ever, we knew we needed to seek the Lord's direction in order to represent Him effectively at such a critical time in our nation's history.

The Lord answered my prayers very specifically as I read the account of Jesus' encounter with the woman at the well (John 4). He taught me by His own example how we are to minister to individuals in our day.

The questions we must ask ourselves are these: How are we doing? Do those around us know we really care? Are we accurately representing Christ and His love to them?

As a result of this study, I coined the phrase "patient evangelism" in order to describe a method that encompasses ninety percent listening and ten percent sharing. While I know this approach is not new, I believe it is something we desperately need to remember as we encounter the world around us. It is a timeless lesson learned during the most extraordinary of times, and most importantly, it is the way that Jesus Himself modeled evangelism.

Studying John 4 made me sensitive to the fact that much of what Christians traditionally do to reach out to the community tends to be contrary to the Lord's example. As I walked around New

York City after 9/11, I noticed a lot of Bible tracts littering the sidewalks and many believers wearing bold Christian T-shirts; but what I did not see enough of was direct, personal ministry to hurting individuals. One of the greatest lessons I learned from the Lord during this time was that as we seek to reach people for Christ, we need to be sensitive to what they are going through — our ministry needs to be responsive to their needs if it is going to be effective.

A few days after the terrorist attack, I was able to put what I was learning from the Lord about patient evangelism into practice. Late one night, our team had the opportunity to begin ministering in lower Manhattan's Union Square Park. The park was teeming with people despite the late hour, and mourners continued to pour in and out of there nearly twenty-four hours a day. Pictures of the missing and cards expressing sympathy for those lost in the World Trade Center lined the walkways. There was a somber atmosphere throughout the park. Candles burned everywhere, bearing witness to the gruesome reality that had just befallen this great city.

As I took in the scene, I noticed a man sitting alone on a park bench with his leg in a cast. Despite all that was going on around me, I was drawn to speak to him, so I walked over and introduced myself. I asked him if he had been in the World Trade Center on 9/11. He said that he worked there and had been in his office that morning. So I sat down and asked him to share his experience with me.

Francis worked on the 26th floor of one of the towers. He was going about his normal routine when, all of a sudden, a violent explosion racked the skyscraper. At the time, he did not know what had happened, but it was like nothing he had ever experienced before. He knew that he needed to get out of there as quickly as possible, so he made his way down the crowded staircase. Before he could safely escape, however, the building began to collapse. Steel and debris rained down all around him, and thick smoke hampered his ability to see. In the end, his leg was broken, but he was still alive.

Nevertheless, the worst part of his harrowing experience was not his broken leg, but the brokenness in his heart. His world had come crashing down along with the building that day. Thousands had been killed, yet he was spared. Like so many others that lived through that awful experience, he was not able to make any sense of it.

As I was listening to his story, I found it easy to share the love of Christ with him. I told him who I was and why I was there, and I began to help him come to grips with some of his questions. Afterwards, I realized that had I just walked over and handed him some Christian literature, he would never have known that I really cared about him. I also realized that as the Holy Spirit led Jesus to the woman at the well in John 4, He had also led me into the park that night to meet Francis. In doing so, God taught me, in a very real way, how patient evangelism actually works.

Since then I have thought about how there are undoubtedly many others who, like Francis, have stories to tell and need to know that someone cares. September 11th was one day that affected us all, but every day there are those around us who are experiencing levels of personal devastation equal to or greater than what was experienced then, only nobody knows. We must ask ourselves, are we really reaching these people? Are we really listening?

Through this book, I want to share with you some of what we experienced in New York after 9/11, as well as some of the lessons we learned through those experiences. But before you go on, I would like to take a moment and ask you to examine your heart. Before we can share the love of Christ with others, we need to experience His love in our own lives personally.

Do you know Jesus Christ as your personal Lord and Savior? Have you ever asked Him to be the Lord of your life? If your answer is no, or if you are not sure, take a moment right now to pray and ask Him to come into your life. Even if you have done this in the past and have walked away, you can pray and rededicate your life to the Lord at this time.

God, I am truly sorry for my sin. I thank You for sending Your Son, Jesus Christ, to die for me in order to pay the penalty for my sin. I want to turn from my self-directed life right now and ask You to be my Lord and Savior. Please come into my life and forgive me. Restore me and make me a new creation; fill me with Your Holy Spirit. Thank You, Lord. In Jesus' name I pray, amen.

If you just prayed that prayer for the first time, welcome to the family of God! You are on your way to a new life in Christ. The Bible tells us, "Therefore, if anyone is in Christ, he is a new creation; old things have passed away; behold, all things have become new" (2 Corinthians 5: 17).

Now, let us look at what the Lord has to say about sharing our faith with others.

The Events of September 11th

CHAPTER TWO

During our Tuesday morning staff meeting on September 11th, I heard that a plane had crashed into the World Trade Center. The staff and I quickly turned on the local news and watched in horror as another plane struck the second tower. We prayed for God's protection over our nation and for the comfort of those who lost loved ones. But as the morning went on, the news kept getting worse. Unbelievably, jets filled with passengers and fuel continued to plummet from the sky—one hit the Pentagon and another crashed into a field in Pennsylvania—and the stalwart towers, so familiar to us all, crumbled to the ground.

Like everyone else that day, I did not understand all that was happening or how far this was going to go, but as the events of September 11th unfolded, the Spirit of God impressed two things upon my heart:

1. From this point on, everything we were going to do as a church was going to change; and

2. Somehow, God would turn even this evil for good.

I have to admit, especially in light of the real possibility of further terrorist activity, it was hard for me to see how anything good could come from such an awful tragedy. And in the midst of the horrifying images that we were seeing—the total devastation and enormous loss of life—it was equally difficult for me to understand in what ways the Lord would want to use our

Amidst the uncertainty, we made a definitive decision—we would focus on the Lord and simply ask Him what He wanted us to do.

church at "such a time as this" (Esther 4:14). But amidst the uncertainty, we made a definitive decision—we would focus on the Lord and simply ask Him what He wanted us to do.

That morning, just moments after we witnessed the second plane crashing into the World Trade Center, I told the staff, "Today our ministry changes forever. It is no longer going to be 'business as usual.'" Immediately, we began to mobilize in order to fulfill our responsibility to bring comfort, guidance, and the Gospel to the people of New York and New Jersey.

Ministry in New York City

As I digested all that was going on around me, my thoughts kept reverting back to the previous day when I was in New York City, playing tour guide at the Empire State Building with our guest from Israel, Amir Tsarfati. Amir, a former captain in the Israeli Army, had been our guide when we were in Israel just one month earlier.

He had come at this time to educate us about the escalating conflict in the Middle East. As we looked at the World Trade Center from the top of the Empire State Building that day, we discussed the terrorist attack that had taken place there in 1993 and our vulnerability to such future attacks. Little did we know how prophetic that conversation would prove to be. In retrospect, it was clear that God was preparing us for what was going to happen.

It was also clear that God had orchestrated the timing of Amir's visit as well. In advance of his arrival, it had been arranged that the two of us would be guest hosts on a live call-in program, which is broadcast on a local New York City Christian radio station. As divine appointments go, we were scheduled to host the program for none other than the afternoon of September 11th. Our topic was to be terrorism in Israel. We now had an additional topic — terrorism in America.

27

Fortunately, the radio station operates from a location in north Jersey, which made it possible for us to get there that day. Despite all the speculation of additional threats and the sheer absurdity of trying to get anywhere near New York City at this time, we prayed and set out on our way, believing strongly that the Christian community needed to bring hope and encouragement to the area.

As we drove north towards the radio station, the unbelievable sight of the New York City skyline—now veiled in the dark, black smoke of destruction—caused us to think, once again, of the example of Queen Esther. Like us, Esther had found herself strategically positioned in a place of influence at a critical time in her nation's history. And, like her, we knew that we could not possibly remain silent! After all, we have also "come to the kingdom for such a time as this" (Esther 4:14).

The Lord opened an incredible door of ministry for us through that radio program. We were exactly where He wanted us to be, doing exactly what He wanted us to do. Not only did we have an opportunity to pray with the station's beleaguered staff, but also, as emergency sirens screamed through the streets of Manhattan, we were able to answer phone calls from many residents whose world had been shaken by the attacks.

God had given us a chance to offer hope through His Word to those most closely affected by this tragedy. We were sharing the Word of God live on the airwaves in New York City on September 11th. We know that only God in His infinite wisdom and mercy could have worked that out!

Ministry in New Jersey

While we were at the station taking calls, the church staff was busy as well. A prayer meeting was scheduled for later that night, and the staff was coordinating a response effort to help meet the needs arising as a result of this emergency. They also gathered information about the well-being of a number of people from within the fellowship who worked in or around the World Trade Center. There was a real possibility that some of them may have been killed. However, as the day wore on, we were grateful and amazed to learn that none had actually lost their lives! Each had a story to tell, and some had extraordinary reasons why they were not in their offices at the time. One had been called out of town on business, another had actually lost his job one month before, someone else was running late that morning, etc.

One man from our fellowship had a very close encounter with death that day. He was on the 92nd floor of the second tower when the first plane hit. He watched the whole thing as it happened, and he immediately headed downstairs. As you can imagine, chaos was abounding. Rescue workers tried to evacuate the building, while security personnel tried to keep people from leaving. They assured the panicked office workers that they did not have anything to fear. "This building is secure," they said, as they urged the people to stay in their offices!

Some listened and returned, but the man from our congregation, encouraged on by another office worker, kept on going down the stairs. By the time they had reached the 40th floor, they felt the building shake as it reeled from the impact of the second jet slamming into their tower. He made it out just as the building began collapsing around him. We praise the Lord for keeping our brother safe, and trust that God will help him as he deals with the incredible effects of this trauma.

On the evening of 9/11, the prayer meeting at the church was packed. I read a prayer of confession and repentance from Daniel 9, which moved me because Daniel had prayed this prayer on behalf of his nation which, because of its rebellion towards God, had now come under His divine judgment. But Daniel knew that although the people were guilty, the great and awesome God whom he loved was merciful and forgiving.

So based not on the righteousness of the people, but on the knowledge of the character of the God he served, he lifted up this powerful prayer of intercession for the people.

As we entered into prayer that night, the requests that Daniel made so long ago resonated within our own hearts as we confessed before the Lord and lifted up our nation to Him. We prayed for all those who were missing and their hurting family members, for President Bush and his advisors, and even for the Muslim terrorists and their salvation. I have to confess that I found it difficult to pray for our enemies — my heart was hard. But God's Spirit moved through His people that night, revealing to us how He wanted us to pray at that time. We also sought the Lord for His direction and asked that He would use us to reach the hurting with the love of Christ. As the night drew to a close, we knew that September 11th had changed us all.

> O my God, incline Your ear and hear; open Your eyes and see our desolations, and the city which is called by Your name; for we do not present our supplications before You because of our righteous deeds, but because of Your great mercies.
>
> *Daniel 9:18*

31

The Days Immediately Following

CHAPTER THREE

Wednesday, September 12th

On September 12th, we had the largest attendance ever at our Wednesday night Bible study. Many were trying to make sense of what was happening around them, and all were hungry for answers, hope, and direction from the Word of God.

We began the night with an extended time of prayer. Then Amir Tsarfati, our guest from Israel, shared a message he entitled, "Will there be Peace in Israel (and Peace over All)?" He was able to shed some light on the ancient conflict between the Muslims and the Jews — a topic that had become headline news overnight. Since Muslims were responsible for this horrific attack on the United States, everyone wanted to know what motivated them to commit such atrocities.

Amir explained that America had come under attack in part because of our support for Israel. He educated us about the Muslim mindset and the meaning of "jihad." He was also able to offer us much-needed encouragement and comfort. He understood very well what it was like to live amidst the destruction and fear that we were now experiencing. He called on us to be faithful witnesses during these dark days. His message, although planned prior to 9/11, could not have been better suited for our present circumstances.

There were young and old, backsliders and new converts, all giving their lives to Christ...we were beginning to see how God meant to bring good out of this awful tragedy.

I also shared a message that night from Solomon's prayer in 2 Chronicles 6 and 7. Surely, if there was ever a time that Christians needed to seek the Lord's face and turn from their wicked ways, it was now! During the altar call that night, many responded to the Gospel invitation—more than could fit into the church's follow-up room!

There were young and old, backsliders and new converts, all giving their lives to Christ as a direct result of the tragedy of 9/11. There was no question, the fields were truly "white for harvest" (John 4:35), and we were beginning to see how God meant to bring good out of this awful tragedy.

Thursday, September 13th

A door of ministry opened to us in New York City through the American Red Cross. On

Thursday, a small group from the church was able to help load commuter ferries with supplies for transport into the city. Afterwards, we hitched a ride into town on one of the ferries and caught a cab into lower Manhattan, but we could only get as far as 23rd Street. There, thousands of people lined the streets cheering the rescue workers and relief crews as they went in and out of Ground Zero. Because we had pastoral credentials, we were able to join a medical team and head into Ground Zero ourselves.

What we saw when we arrived there was even worse than expected. The magnitude of the destruction totally overwhelmed the senses. The area was filled with medical personnel and rescue workers who were all working beyond their ability, dealing with a reality none of us would have ever dreamed possible just a few days before. It was surreal. We had several opportunities to encourage, support, and pray with many of the workers as they began what appeared to be months of grueling work.

Later, we made our way to the Family Center, which had been set up at the Armory on 23rd Street. Many gathered there, hoping to learn news about their missing loved ones. There were photographs everywhere of friends and family members with phone numbers and desperate pleas for anyone with information of their whereabouts to call. After seeing Ground

Zero with my own eyes and now looking into the faces of the distraught and grieving victims, the reality of what had happened in New York City hit hard. The raw pain was pervasive, and it cut me right to the core.

Meanwhile, staff and volunteers back at the church continued to organize a massive relief effort. Due to our close proximity to New York City, we knew that many families in our community had been personally touched by this tragedy. From the beginning, it was my vision to provide physical and spiritual support to them. It was exciting to see others catch this vision.

People from the congregation were looking for ways to minister. They were praying and giving their time to help meet needs. They were sharing their faith with their neighbors. Home group leaders were reaching out to provide comfort and encouragement to anyone in their area who was in need. Hundreds of meals were made for the families of those lost or missing in the attacks. Families were graciously opening their homes in an effort to house the numerous teams expected from all around the country, and a tremendous flood of Bibles and other materials were donated in order to equip those who were going out to minister in the city.

As all of these efforts got underway, we realized we were seeing more of the good that God meant to bring out of this tragedy—He was bringing revival among His people. My prayer was that it would be a lasting devotion, and not merely an emotional response that fades away, as Hosea describes:

> ...Your faithfulness is like a morning cloud,
> and like the early dew it goes away.
>
> *Hosea 6:4*

Friday, September 14th

Regularly scheduled events were put on hold for the time being, and mobilization meetings crammed the church schedule instead. Staff, ministry leaders, and home groups met to pray for and map out ways to meet the overwhelming needs around us. We received thousands of books from Calvary Distribution to give out in New York City, including *Comfort for Those Who Mourn* by Chuck Smith, senior pastor of Calvary Chapel Costa Mesa. Ray Pritchard, a pastor and author from Chicago, personally gave us five thousand copies of his book, *An Anchor for the Soul.* Amazingly, a dear brother drove overnight all the way from the Midwest to hand-deliver these books so that we would have them in time for the next few days of outreach in the city.

We were also blessed to learn that Pastor Brian Brodersen, associate to Pastor Chuck Smith, was on his way to New Jersey from

Washington, D.C. to join with us in ministry. Brian, who had been in Washington on 9/11 for a meeting, was unable to get home to California due to the freeze on flights.

Among those who arrived with him were some friends, Scott and Kerry Hasenbalg (who were very eager to be used of the Lord in New York City), as well as Tom Price, a photojournalist and the editor of *Calvary Chapel Magazine*. Tom not only served alongside us in ministry, but also preserved for us (through words and photographs) an historical account of what the Lord's people were doing at Ground Zero and throughout the New York area during those first few weeks of ministry.

As people arrived and plans were made, there was no mistaking it — the Lord was equipping us to meet the greatest need of our time.

Saturday—Sunday, September 15th and 16th

Like most of the churches in America, our weekend services were packed solid after the attacks. I shared a message entitled "For Such a Time as This," based on Esther 4:14, and encouraged the congregation to recognize that this tragedy was a wake-up call to all believers. I told the body, "It is time to give up our self-centeredness and let our lives be a reflection of Christ's love and grace to the dying world around us."

Brian shared a message from Matthew 11, reminding us of the spiritual battle that is being waged in the heavenlies as we live to reflect the love of Christ in our world. He encouraged us never to stop, but to continue sharing the Gospel with tremendous zeal. He said, "God has given us an opportunity now, as His church, to rise to the occasion and to get His message of love out to people." He exhorted us to be steadfast in:

- *Prayer*
- *Denying sinfulness*
- *Demonstrating love*
- *Proclaiming the truth of the Gospel*

Again, the response we saw from the congregation was tremendous. Many came forward to receive Christ or to rededicate their lives to Him.

That afternoon, Brian and I went into Manhattan where we were trained by Samaritan's Purse in Critical Incident Syndrome Counseling. We were now official Red Cross chaplains.

Monday, September 17th

On Monday morning, a group of us once again headed into the city. Brian and I went uptown to the Plaza Hotel where Cantor

Fitzgerald—a company that lost nearly seven hundred employees in the World Trade Center—had opened a resource center for all of the families of its missing employees. There, we had the opportunity to listen to and encourage a number of people. Nevertheless, we found that we were limited in our effectiveness because there were so many official chaplains on hand to counsel the families. The overabundance of counselors made it difficult for us to really make an impact.

Later on, we met up with the rest of our group. The Hasenbalgs told us that they had spent the entire afternoon ministering in Union Square Park, which is a little north of Ground Zero. The park was filled with people who were looking for hope. Many of them had become displaced by the attacks and were unable to return to their homes in lower Manhattan; others had come there to seek information regarding those who were still missing and to mourn the lost.

In fact, thousands filtered through the park to pay tribute to the dead, light candles, and leave behind pictures and words of sympathy. It turned out that Union Square Park—normally a counter-culture niche and a place for protestors—had become the site of the largest makeshift memorial in the city. So we decided that we would all head back up to the park.

When we got there, we sensed that this was the place God was going to use us. People were grieving; they were searching for some kind of meaning in all that had happened. We stayed until midnight talking with many, including some who were actually in the World Trade Center at the time of the attacks. One man told me that he was now terrified of living in New York City, even after being a long-time resident. Another young woman, who had just returned from vacation, was in shock to learn that her home was no longer accessible to her. What happened in her short absence was a reality too difficult for her to comprehend.

This was the scene everywhere in the park that night—it was like an open wound. We truly felt that our goal was to reach out to people one-on-one, to listen to their stories, and to comfort and love them as they mourned. As a result of this approach, they were eager to hear what we had to say and to receive the materials that we had brought with us.

Tuesday, September 18th

The next day, exactly one week after the attacks, I decided to bring some of the church staff into New York City to continue reaching out to the hurting in Union Square Park. I was convinced more than ever that this was where

God wanted us to minister. As usual, the park was filled with people who had hoped to get into Ground Zero, but were unable to due to the heavy security around the area. Access to everything south of that point was still closed off to the general public.

When we arrived, we began our ministry by simply walking around the park, praying with people, and giving away Bibles. As we did this, we noticed a street musician at one end of the park who had managed to draw a fairly large crowd using a simple battery-powered sound system. Like many others who were there that day, his performance captivated us. He seemed to have tapped into something. In a strange kind of way, the familiar music he was playing brought what was so desperately needed — comfort.

As we were taking all this in, he opened up his microphone to anyone who wanted to share either a song or a thought about what had happened. Immediately we saw the opportunity in this to minister to the crowd, and we were thankful that our worship leader, Pete Episcopo, was one of the pastors who had joined us that day. Pete responded to the invitation, went up, and sang "Amazing Grace." Before long, people all over the park were singing with him.

Afterwards I asked the street musician how long he had been there. He told me he had been there for twenty-four hours straight and that he was so exhausted, he could hardly think anymore. So we offered to take over what he had started. To his total amazement, we had acquired a sound system exactly like his, and we were set up within one hour. We told him to go and get some rest and that we would keep this thing going for him. This blew his mind, and he handed it over to us, telling the crowd, "These people are going to keep this thing going! Look, they have equipment, and they have Jesus in their corner!"

So with a round of applause, the street musician left, and we continued to minister in his place. We knew that if we got up there and started preaching right away, we would lose the crowd, so we decided to continue what he had begun by coordinating an open microphone. It was amazing how God controlled it. Many in the crowd came forward, along with a number from our own worship team. Most were Christians, but even those who were not shared many moving stories and songs, which kept drawing hundreds in to see what was happening.

One woman wanted to share an Eastern chant, but knowing we were Christians, she offered to sing an old spiritual she knew instead. People were coming out of the woodwork and clapping as she sang the lyrics to "Wade in the Water." Later, a ten-year-old girl with dreadlocks sang another song that had everyone in tears. One woman shared a heart-wrenching story of how she had to postpone her wedding plans because of the death of her sister's husband in the World Trade Center. She cried and shared a beautiful poem for her widowed sister. We all felt her pain, as if it had happened to us personally. Afterwards, one of the women from our church was able to reach out to her and encourage her with the love of Christ.

Between every third or fourth song, when the crowd had grown to its peak, Brian, another one of our pastors, or I would share the Gospel and announce that there were free books available to encourage anyone who was hurting. The invitation to receive a book proved more effective than distributing them by hand. We gave away over twenty-five hundred books during the ten hours that we were there. God had once again opened an incredible door of ministry for us in New York City.

By 11:00 P.M., we were as exhausted as that street musician had been when we first came to the park. Amazingly, God provided another group of Christians who had just arrived to continue ministering to the crowd.

As we left the park that night, we reflected on all that had gone on in the last ten hours — the various singers, the young children, the real times of worship, those who shared the Gospel, and the stories of the victims themselves.

Through it all, we saw another glimpse of how God was bringing good out of this tragedy by manifesting His love, in a very real way, to all those gathered in the park that day.

*To Honor
and
Remember*

CHAPTER FOUR

Tuesday, September 25th

About one week after the tragedy, the management of a large performing arts center located in central New Jersey agreed to donate the use of their facility to us for a memorial service. The church staff went to work lining up speakers, putting together materials, and making all the other necessary arrangements needed to host a service in a venue of this size.

On Tuesday, September 25th, exactly two weeks after the attacks, approximately thirty-five hundred people gathered for the memorial service, which we called, *To Honor and Remember.* Family members of some of the victims of 9/11 shared powerful testimonies. Included among them was Al Braca's sixteen-year-old son Chris, who bravely stood before the large crowd and eulogized his father.

Al was one of the seven hundred Cantor Fitzgerald workers lost in the tragedy. Chris spoke of how his father's death was not in vain. He shared the incredible account of the last moments of his father's life, which his family had been able to piece together through e-mails and cell phone calls made from the building that morning. Co-workers who managed to call home to say goodbye to their loved ones comforted their families, telling them that Al had gathered them together and was praying with them. Chris and his family learned that because of Al being there, many received Christ for the first time that morning. Al's family knew it was the way he would have wanted his life to be used. "My dad was an amazing man," Chris said. "He taught me how to love, he taught me how to be a man of God, and he never compromised his faith."

Lisa Beamer also came and shared about her husband Todd. Todd Beamer was a believer and a passenger on United Airlines Flight 93. He became an instant hero, along with the rest of those on the ill-fated flight, when it crashed in a field in Pennsylvania. Todd and others on board managed to stop the hijackers from using their plane as a guided missile in the attack being waged on America that day, and it cost them their lives.

Lisa, who was expecting her third child when her husband died, also became a household name after the attack. Included in what she shared with us that night was the account of her husband's last moments, as relayed to her by an operator who spoke to him that morning. It had been a comfort to her to know that as Todd prepared to fight the hijackers, he had prayed and drawn strength from the Lord.

A member of our own fellowship, Andy Deane, also shared his harrowing experience. Andy, a first-year student at New York University, heard the news of the attack shortly before he received a phone call from his mother, who wisely urged him to get out of the city. Instead of listening to her though, he headed straight to the World Trade Center. He was standing right beneath the burning buildings taking pictures when the first tower collapsed.

He saw a number of firefighters lose their lives, and he himself just barely made it out of the area. The cloud of smoke and debris limited his ability to see or breathe very well, but he found refuge, along with about thirty others, in a small candy store. As the store filled with smoke, it became clear that they could not survive there much longer. Andy prayed that God would use him, and He did.

He shared the incredible account of how God gave him the courage, strength, and wisdom to lead those people to safety and to stay and help the firemen rescue many others. He also shared how God spared his life once again as the second tower came crashing down around them.

We heard testimonies from other survivors as well. Mike Hingson shared how he made it out alive, despite the fact that he was blind and on the 86th floor when the attack occurred. He gave thanks to a firefighter, his seeing-eye dog, and most of all, to the Lord for his survival. Jerry Sillcocks, of Firefighters for Christ in New York City, shared his experiences. Other rescue workers also shared how God had been faithful to them on 9/11 and the days that followed.

Through all the testimonies, Jesus was glorified, and as each testimony was completed, those gathered stood to applaud the survivors' courage and God's faithfulness.

> *Through all the testimonies, Jesus was glorified, and as each testimony was completed, those gathered stood to applaud the survivors' courage and God's faithfulness.*

In addition to the powerful testimonies, Jean-Luc Lajoie of *The Kry*, a duo from the band 7:22, and our own worship leader, Pete Episcopo, led the audience in worship.

Mike MacIntosh, senior pastor of Harvest Christian Fellowship in San Diego, presented the Word of God to the crowd. Mike had been in New York since 9/11 serving in a leadership position for the American Red Cross. He shared a powerful message of the hope we have in Christ. As the service drew to a close, I exhorted all those gathered to remember that while all things are not good, "all things work together for good to those who love God, to those who are the called according to His purpose" (Romans 8:28).

It was an incredible night—lives were changed. There was such a sense of hope and joy. One Congresswoman in the crowd noted that this had been the best tribute of them all. After the service, I had the opportunity to speak with a Japanese news reporter who had been visibly touched by the memorial. I knew he wanted to talk more, so we arranged to meet again, and at that time, I answered his questions and shared the Gospel with him.

Through the memorial, God had opened another incredible door of ministry for us to share the hope of Jesus Christ to those who were most affected by this tragedy. Yet, somehow I sensed that our post-9/11 ministry had just begun.

Ministry Redefined

In those early days, when our usual methods of evangelism and outreach seemed inappropriate in light of the great needs around us, the Spirit of God gave us a fresh approach. He showed us how to focus on reaching individuals.

People were frightened and looking for God, and there were many who made professions of faith. How I wish I could say that the heightened need and desire for God, which was realized during those days, has continued, but unfortunately, it has waned. Sadly, it seems as though many of those who came running back to the Lord, for fear that the "end of the world" was just around the corner, have slowly faded away. They have once again allowed complacency to creep back into their daily routines.

However, what we learned during those days remains and has become known as patient evangelism. Patient evangelism is comprised of a few simple guidelines that can be applied to all of our relationships with unbelievers. The following chapters outline these five main points, which were gleaned from carefully observing how Jesus Himself reached out to a Samaritan woman in His day.

Philosophy
of
Ministry

CHAPTER FIVE

Patient Evangelism Defined

Patient evangelism is a term that was coined to describe the philosophy of ministry we embraced during those first days of outreach following the attack on the World Trade Center. At that time, we were faced with a challenge that we had never encountered before. Reaching people with the Gospel in the midst of such dire circumstances was totally unique.

We found that what had worked in the past—handing out tracts and preaching on street corners—now seemed self-serving, almost as though we were taking advantage of a bad situation. We saw that what was missing from those traditional approaches was an element of genuine concern. After 9/11, we realized that we were dealing with people whose lives had been suddenly shattered. In one day, they had become painfully acquainted with loss, grief, and their own mortality. What they needed now was to know that someone cared about them—they needed to know Jesus!

So the challenge and the prayer of my heart became, how would Jesus want us to reach out to them? How would He have encountered them if He were here with us? Would He have donned a Christian T-shirt, emblazoned with religious symbols? Would He have handed out tracts to passersby while asking them to consider where they would be eternally had they been in the World Trade Center that morning? Or would He have taken the time to really reach people? Would He have learned their names and gotten to know them personally? How would He have shown them that He really cared? How would He have led them to understand their greatest need of all?

I truly believe that if Jesus were here today, He would approach the world in a very different way than we typically do. That is why I wanted whatever we did after 9/11 to be led solely by His Spirit. So as I prayed for guidance, the Lord put John 4 on my heart, and it was from that passage of Scripture that He showed me how we are to reach out to the hurting world around us. Jesus' example became our model for ministry. It is from Him that we learned the lessons of patient evangelism.

A Genuine Concern for Others

We began our times of ministry in New York City's Union Square Park by simply walking around and observing the scene. The park had become the gathering place for thousands who were grieving and seeking answers. Other religious groups were also there, but a lot of what we saw them doing did not reflect the love of Christ, and I did not want us to make the same mistakes.

One such incident took place as we were watching a few young Christians playing music and sharing the Gospel. A man stopped to listen, and they began talking with him. Then a Buddhist, dressed in his religious garb, approached them, asking questions about Christianity, and the discussion soon became heated. Before long, the Christians lost their patience and began arguing with both of them.

At this point, we walked over and began to speak to the man who had stopped to listen in the first place. During a brief conversation, we learned that he had just lost five of his friends in the World Trade Center. This guy was grieving! And what is really sad is that those Christians, who were trying to reach this man, did not even know. They never took the time to ask. This man's pain was so great, and all they were interested in doing was proving that they were right.

What they did was so characteristic of the error that we so often make when we seek to share the Gospel. Although I give them credit for being there and wanting people to know the truth, the problem was that they had totally forgotten about ministering to the person in need. They were more concerned with convincing him—even to the point of arguing—than they were with listening to him. Had they just shown genuine concern, they would have understood that what this man needed was someone who cared, someone who could offer real hope in the midst of this despair. This man needed Jesus, but instead, he got a religious debate.

That is why I wanted everyone who came out to minister with us to spend some time just walking around and observing what was transpiring in the park. We were not there to push an agenda. We were there to offer hope to the despairing and to represent Jesus Christ. The only way we could effectively do that was by showing a genuine concern for others.

Jesus Encounters a Woman in Need

Jesus gave us a great example in John 4 of how we are to encounter those around us.

> Therefore, when the Lord knew that the Pharisees had heard that Jesus made and baptized more disciples than John (though Jesus Himself did not baptize, but His disciples), He left Judea and departed again to Galilee. But He needed to go through Samaria. So He came to a city of Samaria,

which is called Sychar, near the plot of
ground that Jacob gave to his son Joseph.
Now Jacob's well was there. Jesus therefore,
being wearied from His journey, sat thus
by the well. It was about the sixth hour.
A woman of Samaria came to draw water.
Jesus said to her, "Give Me a drink."

John 4:1-7

This familiar story of the woman at the well
took on a rich new meaning for me during our
post-9/11 ministry. The lessons revealed during
that time are relevant to all we do for Christ,
whether in a crisis situation, as in New York
City, or in a chance encounter at the marketplace.
People are in need all around us, and He has
shown us in this passage what He would do if
He were here in the flesh to minister to them.

Samaritans were considered second-class
citizens by their Jewish neighbors because they
were a mixed race of people—having both
Jewish and Gentile ancestry. For this reason,
there was animosity between the Samaritans
and the Jews. This prejudice was so great that
even though the most direct route to Galilee was
through Samaria, the Jews would travel out of
their way in order to avoid the area.

Nevertheless, Jesus ignored this cultural
norm and chose instead to go through Samaria

on His way to Galilee. In fact, the text says, "…He *needed* to go through Samaria," because the Holy Spirit was leading Him there for a purpose.

When Jesus arrived at the well, it was the "sixth hour" (which would have been noon), but more importantly, it was just as a woman was coming to draw water. Although to us this does not appear to be strange, this was actually quite unusual in that day. Normally, the women of the town would have come to the well much earlier, *before* the heat of the day. They would also have come in a group, not alone, as this woman did.

Jesus would have observed this peculiarity and known from it that she was an outcast, rejected by the other women in her community. Yet, He spoke to her anyway, asking her for a drink. Why did He do that? He could have gotten His own water; He really did not need her to give it to Him. Instead, Jesus used His thirst as an opportunity to reach this *thirsty* woman; He connected with her over a common need. He reached out to her because He knew her greatest need was not to fill her empty waterpots, it was to fill the emptiness in her soul.

As I read the Gospels, I am always fascinated with the way Jesus deals with individuals. When I see the Son of God going to this extreme to speak to one lonely woman, my Christian walk is challenged. God has time for the "dregs" of society — the ones who are cast aside and hurting and the ones that cannot help themselves. The searching question is: Do I?

I am also challenged by the way He goes about engaging this woman. He does not assault her with the facts. Instead, He is patient. He gently comes into her life through an open door. He begins a conversation with her that is sensitive to her situation but, as we will see, will ultimately lead to the salvation of many. He shows a genuine respect and concern for her, without being distracted from His sole purpose of meeting her greatest need.

God has time for the "dregs" of society — the ones who are cast aside and hurting and the ones that cannot help themselves. The searching question is: Do I?

Jesus was not looking for confrontation. If that was the case, He could have stayed and debated with the Pharisees over His ministry. Jesus was looking for that *thirsty* woman, and He found her at her place of need. He used her temporal need for water to show her what she truly required — eternal life.

As Christians, this is our calling as well. We are to forget our prejudices and comfort zones and truly reach out in love to the people around us. Do you know the needs of the people in your life, the ones you are trying to win to God? Do you have a genuine concern for them? Do you respect them? Do they think that you really care about them, or do they just feel like they are some kind of project to you?

No matter how wonderful and exciting we know the Gospel to be, we will never be able to share it effectively with a person who feels that we do not respect them or care about their needs. Through His approach, Jesus let this woman know that He respected her. He entered her world, and that led her to enter His.

S.H.A.R.E.

Patient Evangelism Outlined

CHAPTER SIX

The Five Main Points of Patient Evangelism

In this chapter, as we continue our study of John 4, I will outline the five steps that Jesus took to evangelize this woman and win her to the Kingdom. The lessons learned here are as relevant in our day as they were in Jesus' day, and they have become the motivating force behind all that we do as a ministry. In order to make it a little easier to remember these main points, I developed an acronym using the word **SHARE**:

> *Sensitive to the Spirit's Leading*
> *Help Build a Bridge*
> *Arouse Desire*
> *Reveal Sin*
> *Explain the Plan of Salvation*

SENSITIVE TO THE SPIRIT'S LEADING

The most important factor necessary in any ministry is to know that the Holy Spirit is leading it. The **S** in **SHARE** is to remind us to be sensitive to the Spirit's leading. Other influences, pressures, and motivations can sometimes propel us, but it is only when we are sensitive to the Holy Spirit's guidance that we will experience His power and see people's lives changed. Jesus was led by the Spirit to meet the woman at the well; He did not allow other influences to distract Him from where He knew He needed to be. He set all those things aside and was there when she arrived. This is a challenging example for us all.

The most important factor necessary in any ministry is to know that the Holy Spirit is leading it.

At the time of the World Trade Center disaster, we all knew there was work to be done, but like Jesus, we wanted to be in the right place at the right time. So we prayed, and He answered — guiding us as we depended on Him and not on our own plans. Whether it was where we were to minister, or to whom we were to speak, or even how we were to reach each individual who came across our path, He was faithful to lead us each step of the way. And, we learned through this that although we can never plan what God does, we could be a part of it, if the Spirit is leading us.

Ministry Directed & Empowered by the Spirit

This is the kind of ministry God desires and designs for His people. He wants to reach the lost in our day, and He wants to empower His children to impact the world for Him. His desire is to save souls, revive hearts, and build His Kingdom. So why is it that we see so much ineffective ministry taking place? Where is our power?

I believe the answer lies in part with our approach. Oftentimes there is too much planning and too little patience. We need to learn how to wait on the Lord through prayer. God wants us to be a part of what He is doing, not the other way around. He is not interested in blessing our plans; He is interested in finding someone who will carry out His. So in order to have a powerful ministry, we must first begin in prayer, patiently seeking God's direction and allowing Him to order our steps.

Next, we need to be prepared to minister to those we are trying to reach. When we were in New York City, many of the Christians we saw there seemed unprepared to meet the needs of the people around them. They were insensitive, and because of that, they came across as though they were spiritually superior. This is not the way the Holy Spirit leads! It is unfortunate, but sometimes we forget that it is only by the grace of God that we ever came to the knowledge of the truth ourselves. We need to learn how to extend that grace to others as we desire to minister to them.

We ought to be mindful of the way Jesus spoke to individuals. We learn from His example in John 4 that He was, first of all, led by the Spirit to speak to this woman. Secondly, He humbled Himself and used this meeting as an opportunity to draw close to her, without giving off the impression that He was dealing with a spiritual inferior. Finally, and most importantly, He allowed the conversation to be empowered and directed by the Holy Spirit Who knew this woman's heart.

This kind of patience is one of the hardest things to learn. Keeping quiet and allowing God to show you just what part you are to play in a person's life definitely takes power from above. That is why it is key that the Holy Spirit empowers our ministries. He will equip us and lead us as we seek to do His work. Jesus was just as effective speaking to a crowd as He was with this one woman. In the same way, we too will be effective in any situation when we are sensitive to the Spirit's leading.

Just a Piece of the Puzzle

Often in our desire to see a person saved, we feel that it is our "duty" to share the whole

Gospel with them, lead them in the sinner's prayer, and begin to disciple them—all in one brief encounter. If we do not complete this process, we feel that we have somehow failed God. Maybe some of you can relate to this. Whether at an evangelistic outreach or on the telephone with a friend, many of us feel, from time to time, as though we did not get the whole job done. What we fail to understand is that we may not be the full answer for a person; we may only be a piece of the puzzle.

Think about your own life. How many people did God send into your life before you accepted Jesus? If we are honest, I think most of us would agree that we would not have responded favorably to a pushy Christian telling us that we would go to Hell if we did not do what they said. While we may not see ourselves as being this extreme, when we share our faith with others, we need to be careful that we do not let our eagerness or our pride cause us to become insensitive to their needs. Never let it be said that you were a stumbling block to someone else giving his or her heart to the Lord.

It is of great importance that we are faithful to share the Word of God without compromise, but it is equally important that we share it in His power. If we ask the Holy Spirit which piece of the puzzle we are in a person's life, He will show us how to minister to that person. He will empower us with the wisdom and patience necessary for each situation and individual.

When the Spirit leads us, we will not push people — we will not need to. We will sense whether there is an opportunity there or not.

Again, John 4 is our example. Jesus took time with an individual. He went out of His way to reach this outcast woman and to minister to her. He was patient with her. He could have told her Who He was and that she was going to Hell if she did not trust in Him. Instead, He brought her to the place where she recognized her need for a Messiah. And then, He revealed Himself to her. If the Lord took the time to minister to the need of one woman in this way, surely we should do the same.

When the Spirit leads us, we will not push people — we will not need to. We will sense whether there is an opportunity there or not.

The Apostle Paul also knew this. He was a bold evangelist who preached the Gospel everywhere he went; yet he recognized the need for prayer and guidance from the Holy Spirit. He knew what he needed most was to know where the Spirit was leading. Therefore, in Colossians 4:3-4, he wrote,

> Praying also for us, that God would open to us a door for the word, to speak the mystery of Christ, for which I am also in chains, that I may make it manifest, as I ought to speak.

He also encouraged the Colossians in their ministry, saying,

> Walk in wisdom toward those who are outside, redeeming the time. Let your speech always be with grace, seasoned with salt, that you may know how you ought to answer *each one.*
>
> *Colossians 4:5-6, emphasis mine*

It was not Paul's style to come into a city, get on a soapbox, and start preaching *at* people. The Spirit always led him to where he was supposed to be; and once there, he waited for an effective opportunity to share the Gospel. He prayed and received the Spirit's leading and power everywhere he went, and none of us can deny that his was an empowered ministry.

We learn from both Jesus and Paul something very important about the work of God — it is only effective when it is empowered and directed by the Holy Spirit.

Help build a bridge

Jesus knew that the Holy Spirit had led Him to the well that day. Because of that, when the woman arrived on the scene, He knew she was the one He was waiting for, so He took the next step. The **H** in the word **SHARE** reminds us that we also need to take the next step, which is to build a bridge into another person's life. In our text, Jesus does this by starting a conversation with the woman, asking her for a drink.

In order to appreciate what Jesus is doing here, you have to understand the cultural significance of this act. For us, a man speaking to a woman is an ordinary occurrence. But in those days, a Jewish man would never speak to a woman in public, especially an outcast Samaritan woman. By doing this, Jesus broke through the social barrier that separated them. He built a bridge.

Building bridges can be difficult. Starting a meaningful conversation, especially with a stranger, is challenging. But we learn here that building bridges is a necessary part of reaching others for Christ. Whether in ministry or just daily living, you need to be able to reach across those things that divide you from another in order to have a real impact on his or her life.

Also, the manner in which Jesus approached her is very important. When we come off with a "holier than thou" attitude, it does not help the bridge-building process. But asking for a drink was seen as asking for her help, which in that culture, would have served to elevate her to equality with Him. Because of this, she responded to Him by saying,

> How is it that You, being a Jew, ask for a drink from me, a Samaritan woman?
>
> *John 4:9*

Jesus did not conform to the ways of the world. If He had, He would have ignored her, but instead He treated this woman with dignity and respect. He honored her by building a bridge over a cultural divide. This amazed the woman and opened up an opportunity to have a meaningful encounter with her.

Whether in ministry or just daily living, you need to be able to reach across those things that divide you from another in order to have a real impact on his or her life.

Effectively Sharing Your Faith

This is the challenge that you and I face as we attempt to share our faith with others. In New York City, we found that while we were simply handing out tracts or books in the park, we were not really connecting with anyone. We were not building any bridges. Imagine if Jesus had merely handed this woman a scroll and walked away. It would not have had the same impact in her life or in the lives of those she knew.

We decided to set aside the handouts we had brought in favor of just speaking to people on a one-to-one basis. We asked them what they had experienced on 9/11 and how they were doing now. More importantly, we listened and took an interest in what they were saying. As a result, we had many opportunities to share our faith and distribute materials, which we would not have had otherwise. And, instead of seeming pushy and uncaring, we were actually ministering and meeting real needs. We were building bridges and crossing over into more meaningful conversations, just as Jesus had done.

This is a lesson we can apply in all of our relationships with unbelievers. I know it was a lesson that I learned the hard way in my own family. Perhaps you have had a similar experience. When I first became a Christian, I was so zealous—I wanted everybody to know the Lord! Unfortunately, though, I had become too pushy. Instead of drawing my loved ones to Jesus, I was actually having the opposite effect. I had become obnoxious, and because of all my preaching and nagging, my own sister did not want anything to do with me for about four years. I simply did not understand what real ministry was all about. I was so unlike Jesus!

The Lord genuinely loved this Samaritan woman whom He had just met, and it was this sincere show of love that drew her into the Kingdom. He showed His love for her by accepting her for who she was and respecting her as a valuable human being. I, on the other hand, had not shown that kind of love towards my own sister. I did not accept her for who she was. I did not show any genuine concern for her life. I was only interested in changing her, and that turned her off towards the Gospel and me.

I finally reached a place in my walk with the Lord where I realized how badly I had behaved towards my sister, so I wrote her a letter. In it I told her how much I missed her and how I wanted my kids to know their aunt. I did not mention anything spiritual or reference any Scripture. I just brought her up-to-date on our lives and asked about hers. I wanted her to know that I cared about her—because I really did. A week later, I got a response. She said my letter had moved her to tears. I realized from what she wrote that she had always wanted to be a part of our lives, but was very hurt because she felt more like a "project" than a sister to me.

What severed our relationship was a lack of genuine love on my part. In my zeal, I had built a wall instead of a bridge. God taught me patience through this experience, and He showed me the consequences of the mistake that I had made by trying to hurry along the process and pick unripe fruit in my sister's life.

Patience is indeed a hard lesson to learn, but if God is in it for the long run, we need to be also. Maybe you realize that you too have tried to pick some unripe fruit in the lives of those closest to you. Maybe it is your spouse, your friend, or a co-worker. Learn to be patient and love them right where they are. Come down from your soapbox and become a bridge-builder. You never know. Perhaps by doing this, they may actually want to know more about your life, which in turn, may lead to an opportunity for you to share your faith with them.

Arouse desire

Once you have broken the ice and found common ground by building a bridge, it is important that you keep the conversation alive and interesting in order to take your relationship to the next level. This is the next step in patient evangelism — to arouse desire — and can be remembered by the **A** in our word **SHARE**. Here we see how Jesus does this by responding to the Samaritan woman in a very interesting way:

> If you knew the gift of God, and who it is
> who says to you, "Give Me a drink," you
> would have asked Him, and He would have
> given you living water.

> *John 4:10*

Notice, Jesus does not really answer the question she posed in verse 9, but He also does not come right out and tell her the good news either. Instead, He appeals to her intellect. What He says intrigues her — He has become an enigma to her. Undoubtedly, she wonders who this Man is and what this "living water" could be. She is puzzled and wants to know more. So she replies:

> Sir, You have nothing to draw with, and
> the well is deep. Where then do You get
> that living water? Are You greater than our
> father Jacob, who gave us the well, and
> drank from it himself, as well as his sons
> and his livestock?

> *John 4:11-12*

First, she states the obvious — He could not be talking about real water. Then she challenges His authority — did He think He was greater than Jacob, the patriarch who drank from this ancient well himself? This is just the reaction He desires. He gets her attention and engages her in a thought-provoking conversation. I cannot help but wonder if there is a little smile on His face as He says,

> Whoever drinks of this water will thirst again, but whoever drinks of the water that I shall give him will never thirst. But the water that I shall give him will become in him a fountain of water springing up into everlasting life.
>
> *John 4:13-14*

What a model of patient evangelism the Lord is for us here! Imagine this scene—the mighty Creator of the universe, humbly taking the time to stir up the desire for truth in the heart of one lowly woman. Jesus is teaching us something that we sometimes miss in our enthusiasm to see others saved. The truth of the Gospel cannot be effectively passed on to someone who is not interested. It is incumbent upon us to heed His example if we desire the evangelistic work we do to have an eternal impact on the lives of those we encounter.

Jesus aroused the Samaritan woman's interest—now she wants to know more. This is very important, because unless a person acknowledges that there is something lacking in their lives, they will never see the benefit of a relationship with Jesus Christ. Notice the woman's response.

> Sir, give me this water, that I may not thirst, nor come here to draw.
>
> *John 4:15*

Although you can sense from their conversation that she knew this was not real water, you also can tell that whatever this water represented, she had a thirst for it. It reminds me of a similar conversation that Jesus had with Nicodemus

The truth of the Gospel cannot be effectively passed on to someone who is not interested.

in John 3. Nicodemus is a Pharisee who, like this woman, also became intrigued with Jesus. So he came to the Lord one night, asking questions. Jesus answers him and says,

> Most assuredly, I say to you, unless one is born again, he cannot see the kingdom of God.
>
> *John 3:3*

In the next verse, we see Nicodemus' response.

83

How can a man be born when he is old? Can he enter a second time into his mother's womb and be born?

John 3:4

Here we have a very intelligent man asking a question to which he obviously knows the answer. Doing this was just another way of saying, "I know You do not mean the obvious, so tell me what You are really trying to say?" And this is what we see this woman doing as well.

What is critical for us to learn from Jesus is that He did not make the mistake that we so often do when we seek to share the Gospel with others. He was sensitive to the way the Holy Spirit was working in this woman's life, and He did not confront her before the time was right. With this patient approach, Jesus was successful in stirring up an inner desire in her heart to know the truth.

REVEAL SIN

Once you have established relationships with others and stirred up their interest for the things of God, you need to take advantage of the opportunities that God gives you to lovingly speak the truth to them, otherwise you have missed the point. This is another mistake we make when we witness to unbelievers. If some of us are too zealous and pushy, others are too meek and fearful. We are afraid of rejection, and it keeps us from getting to the point, which is twofold: to reveal sin and to explain the plan of salvation—the final two steps in patient evangelism. First, we must be faithful to address the issue of sin as it is revealed in another's life. We can remember this step by the letter **R** in our word **SHARE**, which reminds us to always reveal sin.

Notice how Jesus takes this conversation to the next level. First, He was able to speak frankly to this woman because He invested time in her and built a relationship with her. He did not just blast her with the error of her ways. He showed her that He cared. He brought the relationship to a place where she was willing to listen. Second, as He speaks the truth to her, He does not do it in a condemning way.

Instead, with words of grace and knowledge, He gently turns the spotlight onto her personal life, saying,

"Go, call your husband, and come here." The woman answered and said, "I have no husband." Jesus said to her, "You have well said, 'I have no husband,' for you have had five husbands, and the one whom you now have is not your husband; in that you spoke truly."

John 4:16-18

85

Imagine for a moment the impact His words must have had on her. He touched the deepest issue of her life—she wanted to be loved! But five husbands had obviously not been the answer, and there was not much hope for this current relationship either. She had been drinking from the wrong well, and her life had become barren as a result. Now she stood before the One who could quench her thirst forever, but there was something that had to be dealt with first—the issue of sin. In essence, what Jesus is telling her here is that the first step in attaining this "living water" is to realize you have been drinking from the wrong well. This is key. A person needs to understand what they are being saved from before they can really appreciate the Savior. They need to acknowledge their sin.

A person needs to understand what they are being saved from before they can really appreciate the Savior.

Call it by its Name—Sin

This woman sought to fill the emptiness in her life with something other than God. This is idolatry, and idolatry is sin. Sin can be subtle, and if we are not aware of its ways in our lives, we will begin to make excuses for it or to minimize it so that it does not sound as bad as it really is. Be careful when you start blaming other people, society, or your past for the choices that you make. No matter how reasonable you try to make it sound, sin is sin, and we need to deal with it completely and stop making excuses for our behavior.

Jesus was faithful to bring her sin to her attention. He was not interested in making her feel better about her circumstances. He was saying to her, "Look how thirsty you are! You went from man to man, and you cannot find any satisfaction. You are looking to the wrong things. I can show you something that will truly satisfy."

People in our world today are on this same treadmill. They are thirsty and drinking from all the wrong wells. They think they will be fulfilled when they get more stuff, make more money, or like this woman, they may think a new spouse will do the trick. So they strive, sometimes at the expense of others, to fill themselves with more of what they think will satisfy. However, it is an endless pursuit—a marathon without a finish line! Oh, for a while, there may be a sense of fulfillment, but ultimately nothing in this world will ever satisfy the thirsty soul aside from a relationship with the living God.

How many of us know people that are extremely wealthy and yet are still searching for something more? They find their money is not much comfort to them when their marriage falls apart, when they lose their health, or when they find that their children are on drugs. That is why Jesus warned us of the deceitfulness of riches. Money makes people think that they are okay, but when the hard realities of life set in, money is just another dry well.

A story I heard recently illustrates the inability of money to make a person happy:

A lady earned minimum wage as a factory worker. One day her boss overheard her saying, "If only I had a thousand dollars, I would be perfectly happy." The boss thought, "Boy, I'd love to see a perfectly happy woman." So he went to her and said, "Here's a thousand dollars, I heard what you said." As he was walking away, he overheard her once again, this time moaning, "Why didn't I say five thousand dollars would make me perfectly happy?"

We can all relate to this, right? Our human nature is never satisfied. We will never have enough. King Solomon, the richest and wisest man who ever lived, said, "the eyes of man are never satisfied" (Proverbs 27:20).

This Samaritan woman went from man to man, thinking it would somehow be different. This man is the one—he is my answer, my hope. But before long, his flaws began to show, and someone else started looking a little better. Her life had become one of seeking and never finding, until this divinely appointed day when Jesus Christ came into her life and gently, but faithfully, pointed out to her, "What you are looking for, you will never find there."

Jesus hit the mark; it is up to her now. How will she handle this issue of her sin? How will she respond? Well, she does something that a lot of us do under similar circumstances — she changes the subject. It is a natural defensive mechanism. When someone gets a little too close for comfort, we tend to want to shift the conversation, taking the focus off us and putting it on to something else. She does this by bringing up the issue of religion.

Sir, I perceive that You are a prophet. Our fathers worshiped on this mountain, and you Jews say that in Jerusalem is the place where one ought to worship.

John 4:19-20

This is a very divisive topic between the Jews and the Samaritans, which could have served to derail the conversation. But Jesus does not get sidetracked here. He keeps His focus on the main thing — her need for salvation.

Explain the plan of salvation

When we are witnessing to others, one of the challenges we face is to avoid entering into a religious debate *with* them instead of explaining the plan of salvation *to* them. That is what the final letter **E** in the word **SHARE** represents. Many times, people we are reaching out to will try to derail the conversation by instigating a religious argument, as this woman's comments could have done. But here we see how Jesus does not allow what she says to cause Him to deviate whatsoever from His purpose. He gets right to the heart of the issue as He answers her.

> Woman, believe Me, the hour is coming when you will neither on this mountain, nor in Jerusalem, worship the Father. You worship what you do not know; we know what we worship, for salvation is of the Jews. But the hour is coming, and now is, when the true worshipers will worship the Father in spirit and truth; for the Father is seeking such to worship Him. God is Spirit, and those who worship Him must worship in spirit and truth.
>
> *John 4:21-24*

From this passage, we see Jesus bring the conversation to the main point (the hour which is to come). He did not allow this divisive issue to turn the discussion into a debate, but instead shifted the focus to something they could agree upon.

Do Not Argue

He does not argue with her even though she was clearly wrong. The Samaritans did not worship God in the right way — they had turned away from the Law. They had developed their own religion, based on their own thinking. It was more convenient for them to worship in the mountains of Samaria than to travel all the way to Jerusalem. So they built their own altars and chose what was convenient over what was right. They mixed in just enough truth to make it sound good and to ease their consciences, but they really were not worshiping the God of the Bible anymore. They had created their own god, according to their own image, and this was whom they now worshiped.

We have a lot of this kind of "high place" religion in America today. People do not realize they are making up their own gods when they say things like, "If I were God, this is what I would do!" But that is exactly what they are doing — creating gods in their own image. They determine for themselves what is right, and they begin to live and serve their own debased standards, rather than the standards established by the true and the living God.

Recent polls show that less than one out of every three adults in America attends church on a weekly basis; and only half of those who say they are Christians actually live their lives based on Biblical truths. That is why people who are unfamiliar with God and who live contrary to His ways will still say to you, "Oh yes, I believe in God." But in whom are they really trusting? Is it the God of the Bible? Or is it just a figment of their own imagination—a god of their own creation? It sounds good and it eases their conscience, but it is really idolatry—the worship of a false god.

So why is it that Jesus does not make the Samaritan woman's religion the main issue? Why does He not set her straight? Why should we, as Christians, not make it our business to tell others how wrong they are in the way they approach God? After all, it is true—they are wrong!

Well, if we are willing to learn, Jesus has something valuable to teach us in the way He handles this. If He had taken a superior attitude, He would have lost the opportunity to get to the real issue—salvation. Instead, the issue would have become proving who is right and who is wrong. She would have been successful in changing the subject. I love how sensitive Jesus is to this. He realizes there is a lot she does not know, so He sidesteps this trap, and instead of needing to prove His point, He offers her something better.

This is where we fail so often as we attempt to share our faith with others. It is the same mistake we observed those Christians in Union Square making. They lost the opportunity with a hurting man because they were more interested in proving they were right than in revealing the plan of salvation. When we begin arguing, we are missing the point, and we lose the opportunity to share truth with a needy soul. Why argue with someone whose doctrine may be off when you have something more to offer them?

Instead of being swayed from the issue by her lack of understanding, Jesus tells her that she is right. The things that divide really are not

> *When we begin arguing, we are missing the point, and we lose the opportunity to share truth with a needy soul.*

important, and pretty soon none of this — wells, places of worship, etc. — is going to matter anymore.

Do Not Avoid the Truth

We also notice from the previous verses that although He does not argue with her, He does tell her the truth. When we begin defending our position, oftentimes we get off track. Here,

Jesus makes it clear that the Jews worship in the correct way, and through that way, salvation will eventually come. Yet, He corrects her in such a way that lets her off the hook — she does not need to fight this battle with Him. He reminds her that the issue is not the style of worship because there is something better coming, and she picks up on that, saying,

> I know that Messiah is coming.... When He comes, He will tell us all things.
>
> *John 4:25*

So now, with a lot of patience and a little bit of gentle, loving correction, her thinking comes around to the real issue. Her response shows the shift that has taken place in her heart as she willingly turns away from what divides them to an issue that they can agree on — the coming Messiah. And as soon as she mentions her hope of a Messiah, Jesus reveals Himself to her, saying,

> I who speak to you am He.
>
> *John 4:26*

His patience paid off. This was the work He had come to do — to win a soul.

S.H.A.R.E. in Review

Jesus showed He cared. And He did not allow divisive issues to create a barrier between Himself and this woman. Instead, He used what they had in common to unify them, bringing the woman to a place where she could hear the truth. That needs to be the focus of all our evangelistic efforts—not to prove we are right, not to make a name for ourselves, not to push our own agendas, but to win a soul for Christ. There is nothing more important than that. So do not waste time arguing with people over *minor* issues of doctrine. All that will be straightened out in time. When you are talking to someone about the Lord, keep it simple, and keep it about the main thing. Keep it about Jesus. And remember these five steps Jesus modeled for us:

1. **S**ensitive to the Spirit's Leading:

   This is the most important factor in any ministry undertaking, and it is the kind of ministry God desires and designs for His people.

2. **H**elp Build a Bridge:

   We need to show people that we care. We do this by reaching across those barriers that divide.

3. **A**rouse Desire:

People are drawn to the truth by their own desire to know, not our desire to tell.

4. **R**eveal Sin:

Before a person can really appreciate the Savior, they need to acknowledge their sin.

5. **E**xplain the Plan of Salvation:

Stay focused. Remember you have something more to offer them — the love of Christ.

Amazingly, all of these steps occurred during a single encounter with Jesus. In most of the experiences I have had, this is rarely the case. Most often, these things take place gradually, over a period of time, as trust is built in a relationship. This is why patience is key. Jesus was not aggressive in His ministry to this woman, He was responsive to her. And because of His sensitivity, her desire grew.

We may not get the opportunity every time we share our faith with another to see each of these things take place. We need to bear in mind that God may be using us to fulfill a specific role in the plan that He has for that person's life. So it is extremely important that we are patient and sensitive to the Lord's leading as we minister the Gospel.

Remember, these steps are not meant to be a magic formula, but they are insights gleaned from the life of Christ Himself on how to effectively share His love in our world.

Lasting Results

CHAPTER SEVEN

The time Jesus spent with this one woman produced a harvest beyond what anyone could have possibly imagined. The disciples certainly did not see it. The text says that when they returned from their journey to Samaria, they were "marveling" at the sight of Him speaking with her. They just could not understand it. And from a human perspective, it did not make sense. But the Holy Spirit had led Jesus to this appointed meeting, and as we read on, we will see how this one transformed life was used to reach an entire city.

> The woman then left her waterpot, went her way into the city, and said to the men, "Come, see a Man who told me all things that I ever did. Could this be the Christ?" Then they went out of the city and came to Him...And many of the Samaritans of that city believed in Him because of the word of the woman who testified, "He told me all that I ever did." So when the Samaritans had come to Him, they urged Him to stay with them; and He stayed there two days.
>
> *John 4:28-30, 39-40*

In her excitement to tell others about Jesus, the woman hurried off, leaving her waterpot behind. After all, she had something much more precious now — "living water." As a result of her testimony, many came out to see Jesus for themselves and believed. They invited Him to stay, and for two days, Jesus ministered in Samaria. During this time, the people of the city became convinced that this Man was indeed the Christ. They told the woman,

God opened a door to an entire city through one conversation with an outcast woman.

> Now we believe, not because of what you said, for we ourselves have heard Him and we know that this is indeed the Christ, the Savior of the world.
>
> *John 4:42*

That is amazing! God opened a door to an entire city through one conversation with an outcast woman. This is the way patient evangelism works. You are led by the Holy Spirit to touch one life, they in turn touch another, and before long, the entire culture begins to change. This is something we need more of today!

The Secret to Lasting Happiness

Right now, I would like to shift gears a little and look at what the disciples were doing during this time. They had left Jesus at the well to go and get some food. When they returned, they found Him talking to this Samaritan woman. They thought this was a little odd, but they did not say anything to Him. After she left, they urged Him to eat. He responds,

I have food to eat of which you do not know.

John 4:32

The disciples were confused by this and started asking each other:

Has anyone brought Him anything to eat?

John 4:33

Jesus explains to them,

My food is to do the will of Him who sent Me, and to finish His work.

John 4:34

Jesus tells them that the food He is referring to is not temporal, but spiritual food. He wants them to understand that the secret to lasting fulfillment and happiness in this world comes from one source—obedience to the will of the Father. This is one of the greatest lessons Jesus ever taught.

In our world today everyone is searching for lasting happiness. But apart from the will of God, the best we can hope for is conditional, shallow, and temporal results. It is only when we discover and choose to live out God's will for our lives that we will be truly satisfied. When we are fulfilling the purpose for which we were created, we will experience no lack.

The Harvest

It is interesting to note that it was into this very city of Samaria that the disciples had traveled for food, and yet they did not seem to notice the spiritual hunger of the residents there. As the people of the city were coming out to meet Jesus, He tells the disciples,

> Behold, I say to you, lift up your eyes and look at the fields, for they are already white for harvest!

> *John 4:35*

It makes you wonder what the disciples were thinking! Had they possibly missed something while they were in the city? Perhaps there was an opportunity to minister, but they did not see it. Maybe they were blinded by their racial prejudice, or perhaps they were just too preoccupied with meeting their own temporal need—finding food. Whatever the reason, they went into the city without Jesus and were unaware that the fields were "white for harvest."

I think that sometimes we miss this point too. We do not realize that the purpose of our lives is to work in these same fields. We get distracted, taking care of all our own needs, and we miss the opportunities that we are given to minister. We need to heed the exhortation that Jesus gave His disciples. We need to ask ourselves the same questions. Have I lifted up my eyes and seen that the fields are already "white for harvest"? Am I missing opportunities to partake of the spiritual food that brings lasting happiness?

When that becomes our desire, as we pray, the Holy Spirit will open effective doors of ministry for us. He will transform our barren lives into productive ones. So put aside the things that are distracting you, and lift up your eyes. Who knows? God might use you to bring about an even greater harvest.

A Harvest
in
His Time

CHAPTER EIGHT

I have to admit that there was a time when I envied those fiery street evangelists. I admired their boldness and fearless courage in preaching the Gospel. The gift God has given some of these preachers truly is to be desired. It enables them to win many souls to Christ, and in such tremendous ways. However, I have become convinced that for most of us, this kind of evangelism can be a lazy approach, and it is not the example Jesus has given to us.

Even Paul the apostle, as bold as he was in preaching the Gospel, never set out indiscriminately. He always prayed for God to open an effectual door through which he could preach, and he faithfully went wherever the Spirit led him, no matter how unimportant it appeared to be on the surface.

For instance, in Acts 16, after spending several days in the city of Philippi (a key city in the region of Macedonia where the Holy Spirit directed Paul to preach the Gospel), he shared the Gospel with just a few women beside a river outside the city on the Sabbath day. Only one of them, a woman by the name of Lydia, actually gave her heart to the Lord as a result.

The amazing thing about this story, like that of the woman Jesus met at the well, is that on the surface, this encounter seemed unimportant in light of the fact that there was such a great metropolis to reach. But with the Lord, every soul won is a victory, and with every victory, new ground is taken for the Kingdom of God.

As a result of Paul's obedience to go to this city and humbly speak to these few women, he found a place to stay in Lydia's home, which ultimately led to his establishing a church there in Philippi. Several years later, Paul wrote a letter to the Philippians that has become part of our Bible today. The Book of Philippians is an encouragement to us all and serves as an example of what God can do when we are obedient to His specific call on our lives.

The Lord was reminding us not to lose sight of the value of one soul in the midst of the great turmoil and need that was all around us.

In the aftermath of 9/11, as we prayed and began planning, it was clear that God had a specific call on our lives as well. He wanted us to make the same kind of personal investment in the lives of the people to whom we would be ministering as He had done with the woman at the well. The Lord was reminding us not to lose sight of the value of one soul in the midst of the great turmoil and need that was all around us. He wanted us to look into their eyes, to feel their pain, and to sense their loss so we could offer them real comfort and hope for the days ahead.

We could not do this by merely preaching the Gospel on street corners and peddling tracts. This truly would have been the lazy approach. If we were to have an effect on our metropolis for the Kingdom of God, we had to walk through the streets of Manhattan, being led of the Spirit, patient, and sensitive to the people He would bring across our path.

While there is no "formula" for reaching the world around us, I believe that Christ has given us the best example we could possibly have. The lessons learned and shared in this book have not faded with time, neither are they relegated just to dealing with tragic situations. Like all good Biblical instruction, they are valuable to all we do and continue to be the foundation upon which we build.

Remember, evangelism is not about just getting out there and doing it; it is about being sensitive to the Spirit and meeting needs. It is about picking fruit in its season and knowing what piece of the puzzle you are. Most importantly, it is about bringing Jesus to the world around us.

That is why this passage in John 4 gripped me so much. As I studied, I felt like one of the disciples, marveling at the unusual sight of Jesus speaking to this hopeless woman. It inspired me in several ways.

1. *Instruction*. This is a rare glimpse into Jesus' personal style of ministry and a good example of how He walked among the people of His day. There is much to be learned from observing this encounter.

2. *Motivation*. I felt we needed to do something different. If Jesus was so sensitive in the way He reached out to this woman, we should do the same. This meant we had to abandon the way we normally would approach an evangelistic outreach in order to be available to minister as He desired.

3. *Empowerment*. The Holy Spirit led and empowered Jesus. That is our greatest need — ministry that is empowered by the Holy Spirit. I wanted that more than anything else. I wanted us to be led and empowered the way Jesus was.

Indeed, we did see the power of God rest on all we did as we implemented these principles. We would have missed countless opportunities to share the Gospel in New York City if we had not yielded to His direction.

Is it Business as Usual?

What happened in New York City on 9/11 impacted the lives of everyone who lived there. Wherever you went in the days following the tragedy, people were talking about it. They had friends or loved ones who were missing, homes they could not return to, no place to go to work anymore, and there was a real sense of shock, horror, and loss.

Along with the devastation came new life. We witnessed it springing up out of the rubble. We know that God will be faithful to produce a harvest there, in His time.

However, when you go into New York City today, you will hardly notice a difference. It seems like business as usual, but that is not really the case. Like the skyline, which has been altered forever, the lives of those who lived through that day will never be the same.

Nevertheless, along with the devastation came new life. We witnessed it springing up out of the rubble. We know that God will be faithful to produce a harvest there, in His time. On the surface, it may seem like good old New York, but we know that it is not. We still encourage those going into New York to ask people about their 9/11 experience, because in doing so, we know that they will have opportunities to share the love of Christ.

In fact, we found during an outreach almost one year later that people were still talking about their experiences. While many, to be sure, are tired of hearing the stories, there are possibly hundreds of thousands who still have stories to tell—some seemingly insignificant and others powerfully moving. If Christians would only take the time to listen, undoubtedly they would hear the cries of a hurting and uncertain world. What better time than right now to begin that bridge-building process in order to share the Gospel with those around you.

Finally, I would like to exhort us all not to lose sight of what real ministry is. In these days of organized outreaches, ministry teams, budgets, and time constraints, there are enormous pressures in the Christian world to "get results." Sadly, many of our ministries have succumbed to this pressure and have become performance-driven. This shift in emphasis has resulted in many individuals being overlooked, or even worse, turned off by what they perceive as pushy, self-serving Christianity.

Oh, that the Lord would slow us down to follow the loving example of patience and sincerity that He has set for us. Remember, you may be a sower, or you may be a reaper, but in whatever you are doing, be patient and sensitive to the Lord's leading, and in the end, we will all rejoice together.

> And he who reaps receives wages, and gathers fruit for eternal life, that both he who sows and he who reaps may rejoice together.
>
> *John 4:36*

Recommended Reading

Apologetics

Know Why You Believe, Paul Little
Know What You Believe, Paul Little
More Than a Carpenter, Josh McDowell
Who Moved the Stone? Frank Morison
Case for Christ, Lee Strobel
Case for Faith, Lee Strobel

Evangelism

A Passion for Souls: The Life of D.L. Moody, Lyle Dorsett
How to Give Away Your Faith, Paul Little
Harvest, Chuck Smith
The Soul Winner, Charles Spurgeon

For New Believers

NKJV Here's Hope New Testament, Broadman
NLT Seeker's Bible NT, Greg Laurie
New Believer's Growth Booklet, Greg Laurie
My Heart, Christ's Home, Robert Munger

Tools for Witnessing

He Did This Just for You, Max Lucado
How Can a Man Be Born Again? Chuck Smith
NLT Gospel of John, Tyndale

Other Materials Available

Visit Calvary Chapel Old Bridge's web site at www.ccob.org for additional information and audio messages by Pastor Lloyd Pulley. Video/ audiotape, CD packages, and Bible studies are also available on-line. You may also contact us by calling 732-679-9222 or by writing to:

Calvary Chapel Old Bridge
123 White Oak Lane
Old Bridge, NJ 08857

DATE DUE